The Melody Of Love

Valentine's Day Coloring Book

Your Love Your Way Just Color It

Anny Will

Happy Coloring⬚

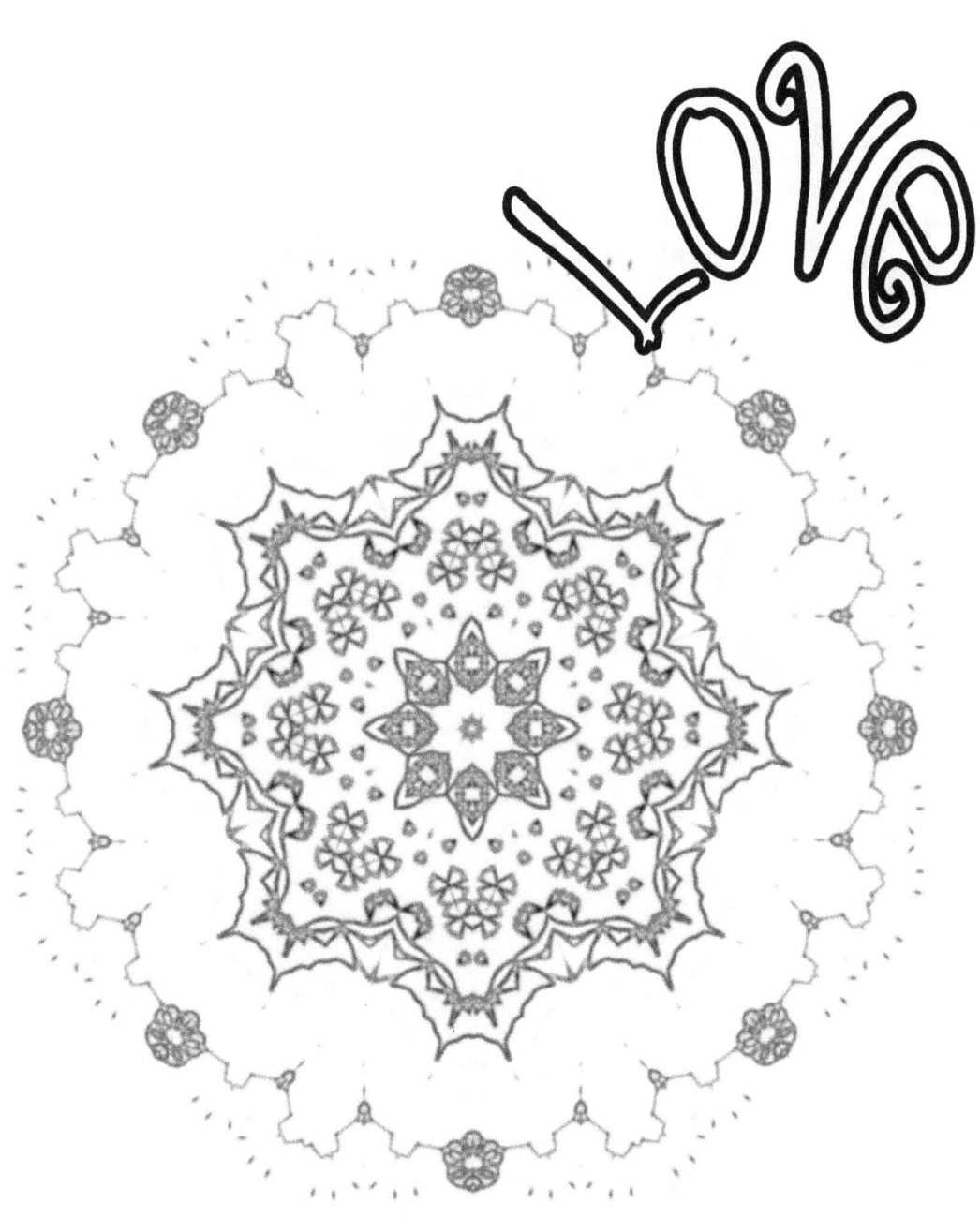

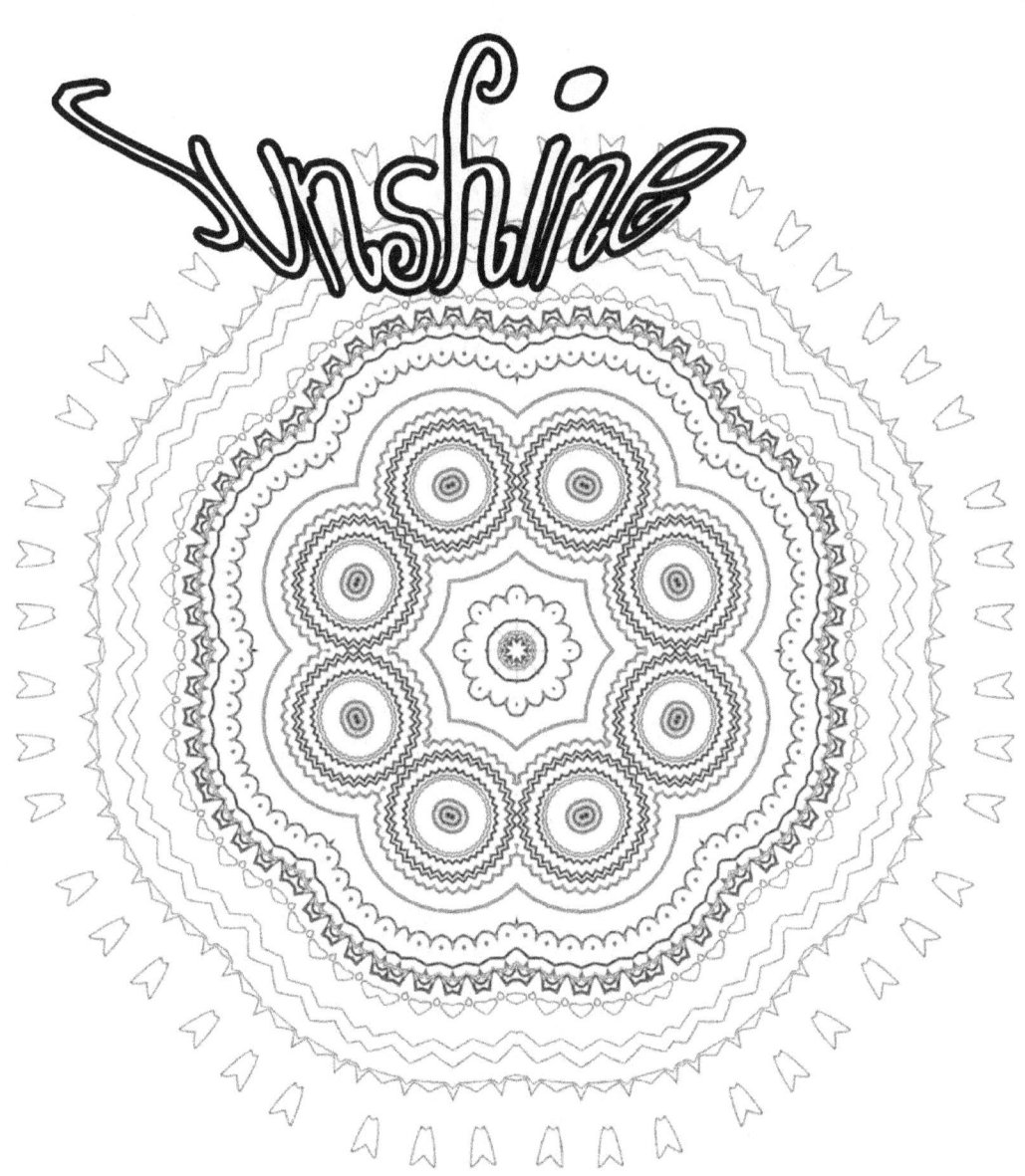

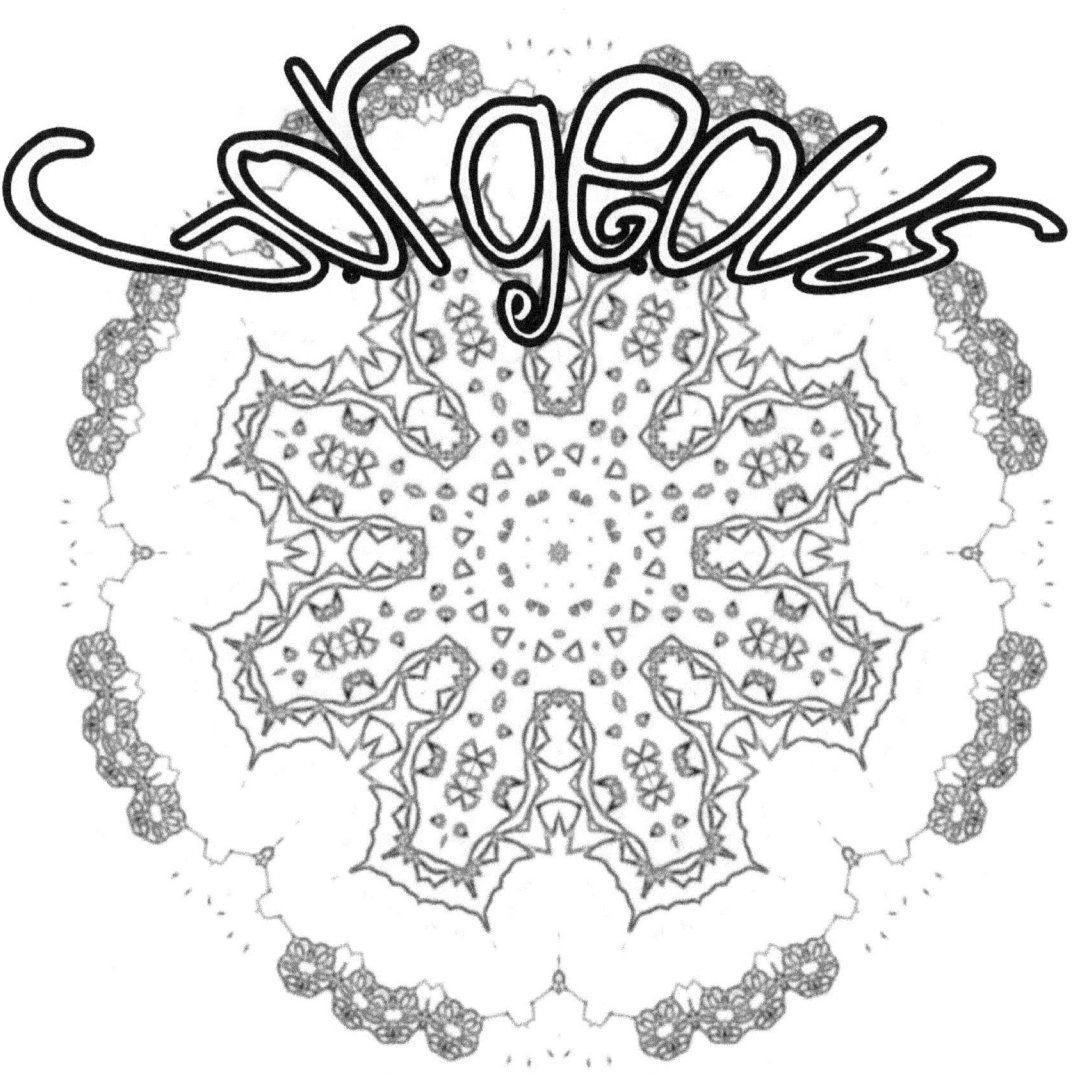

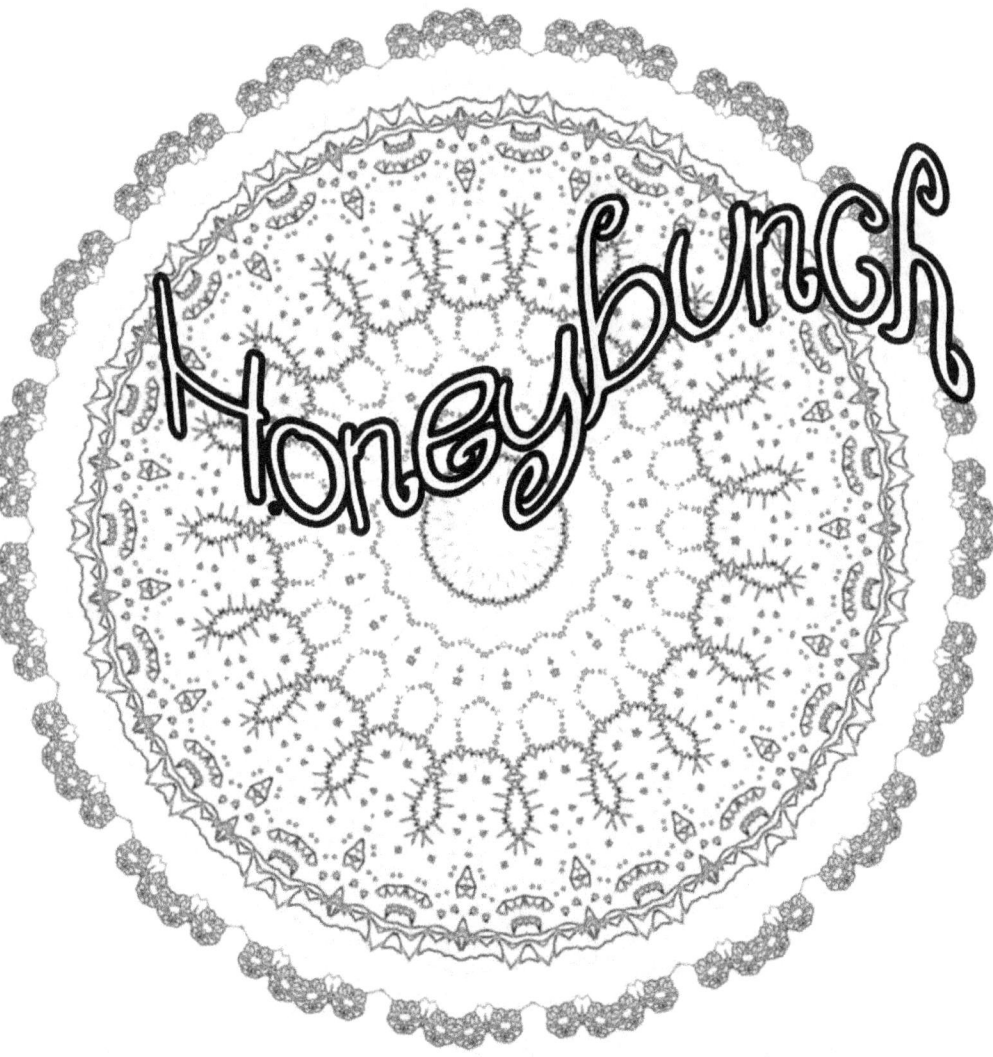

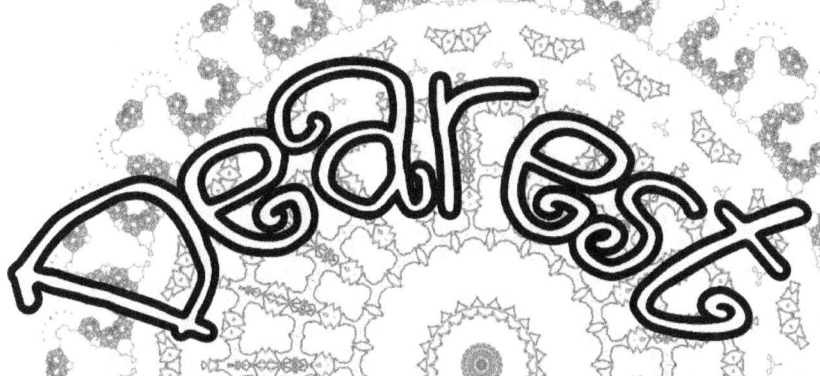

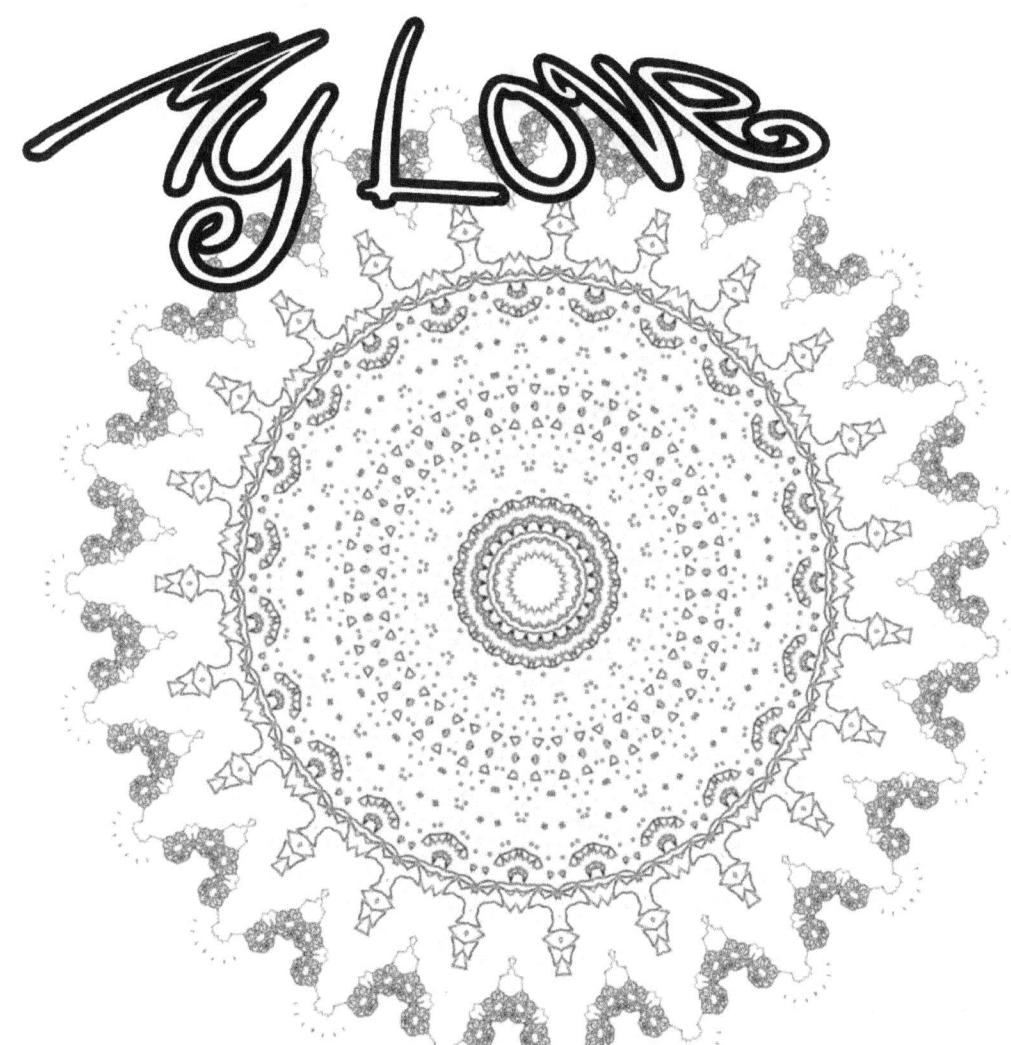

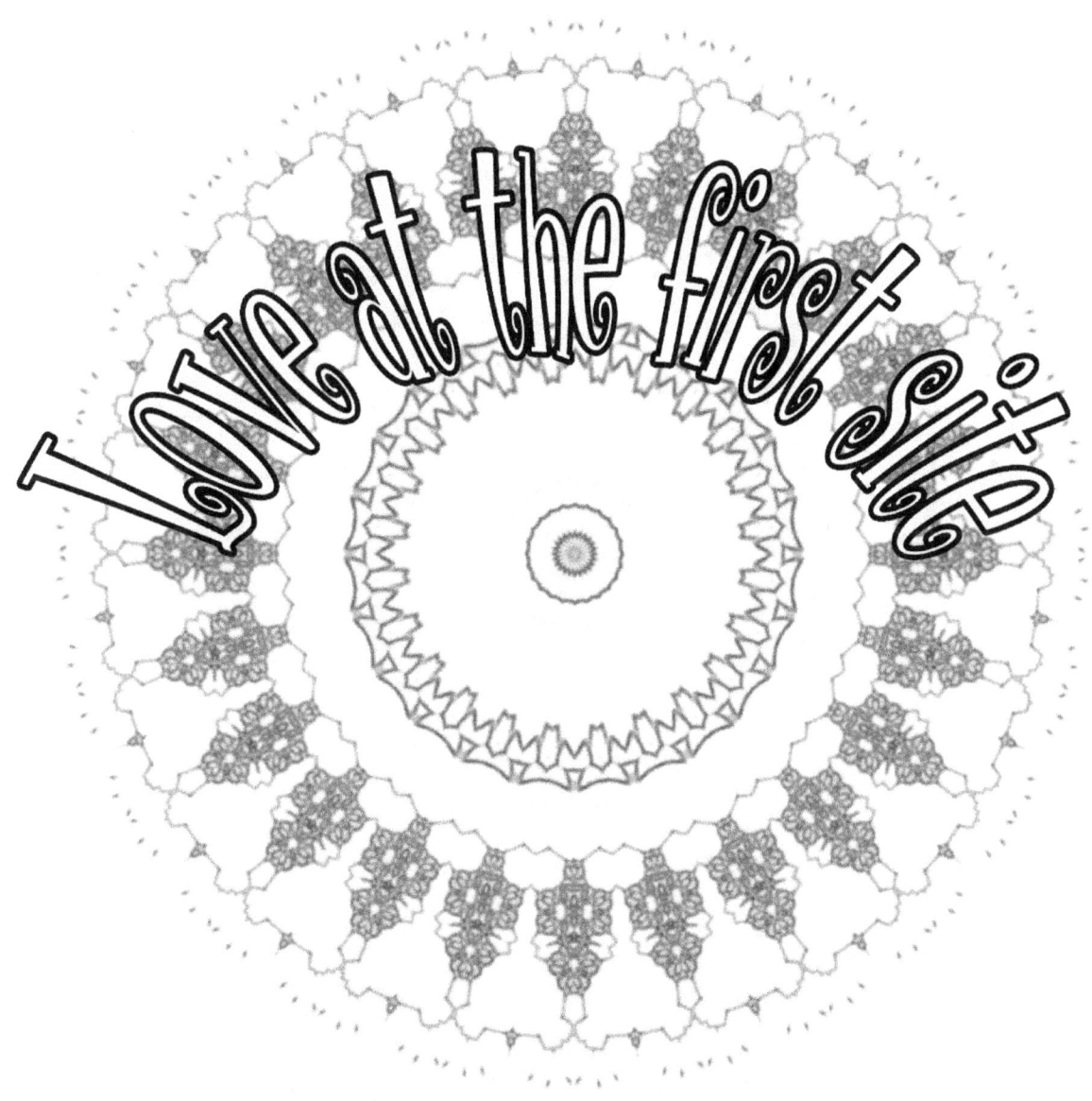

Love at the first site

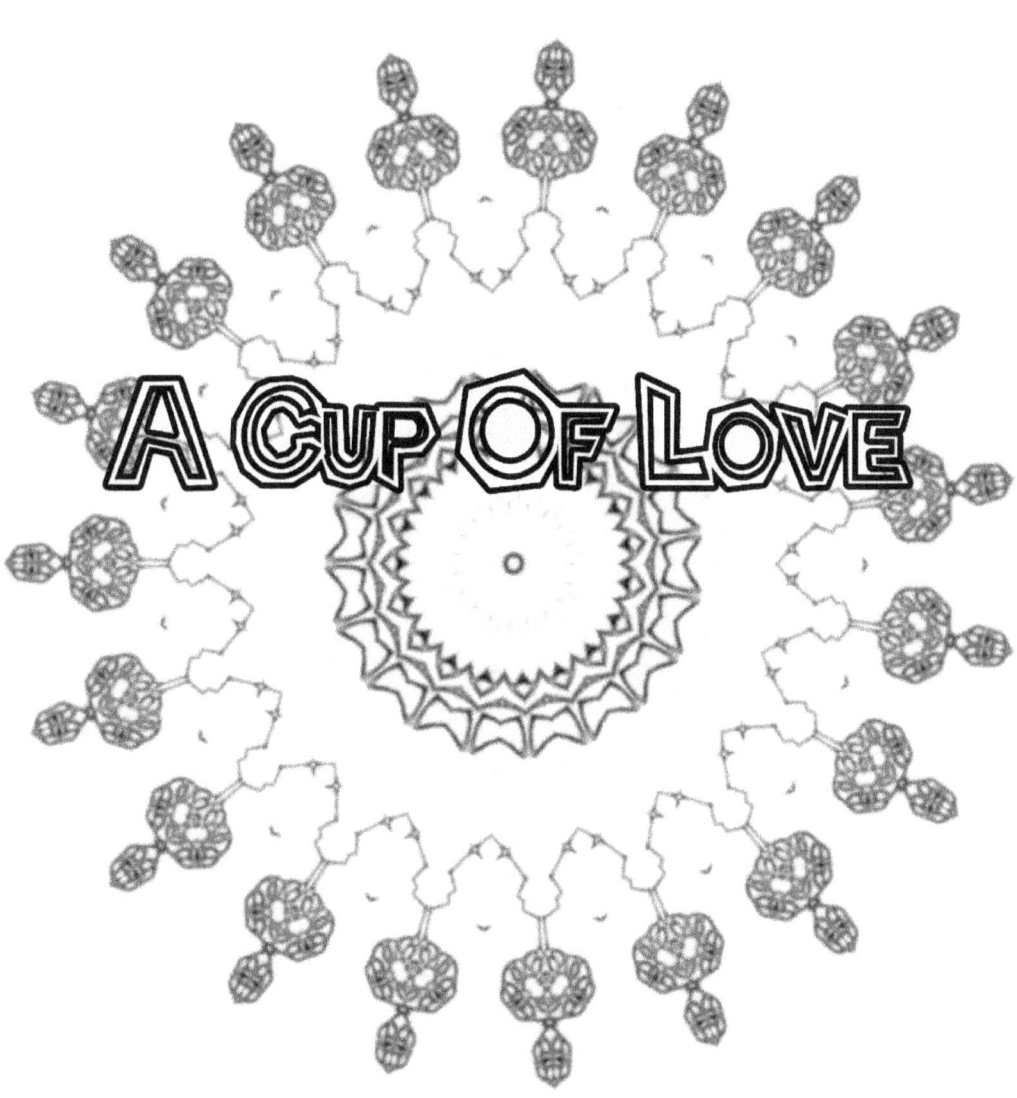

A Cup Of Love

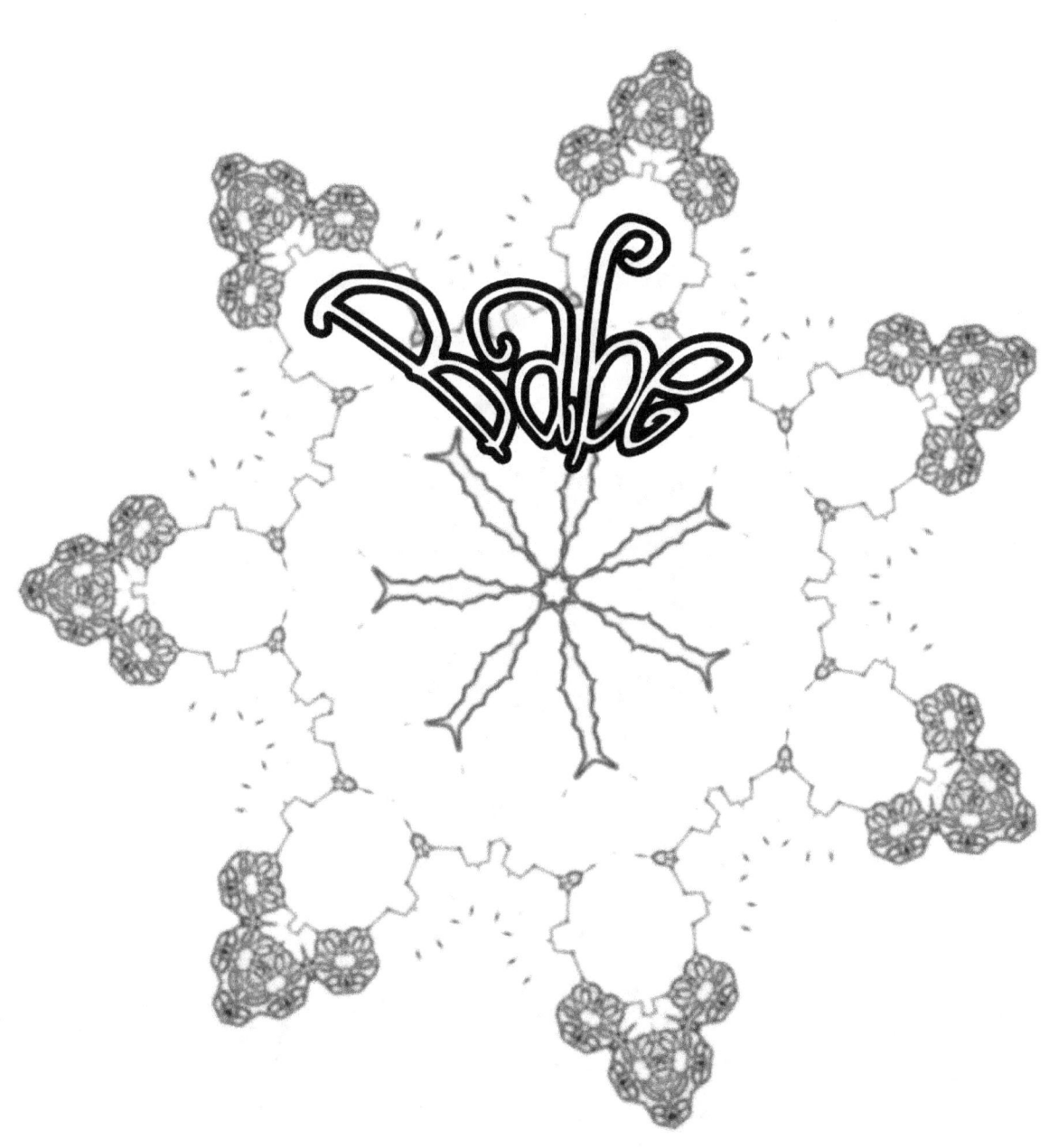

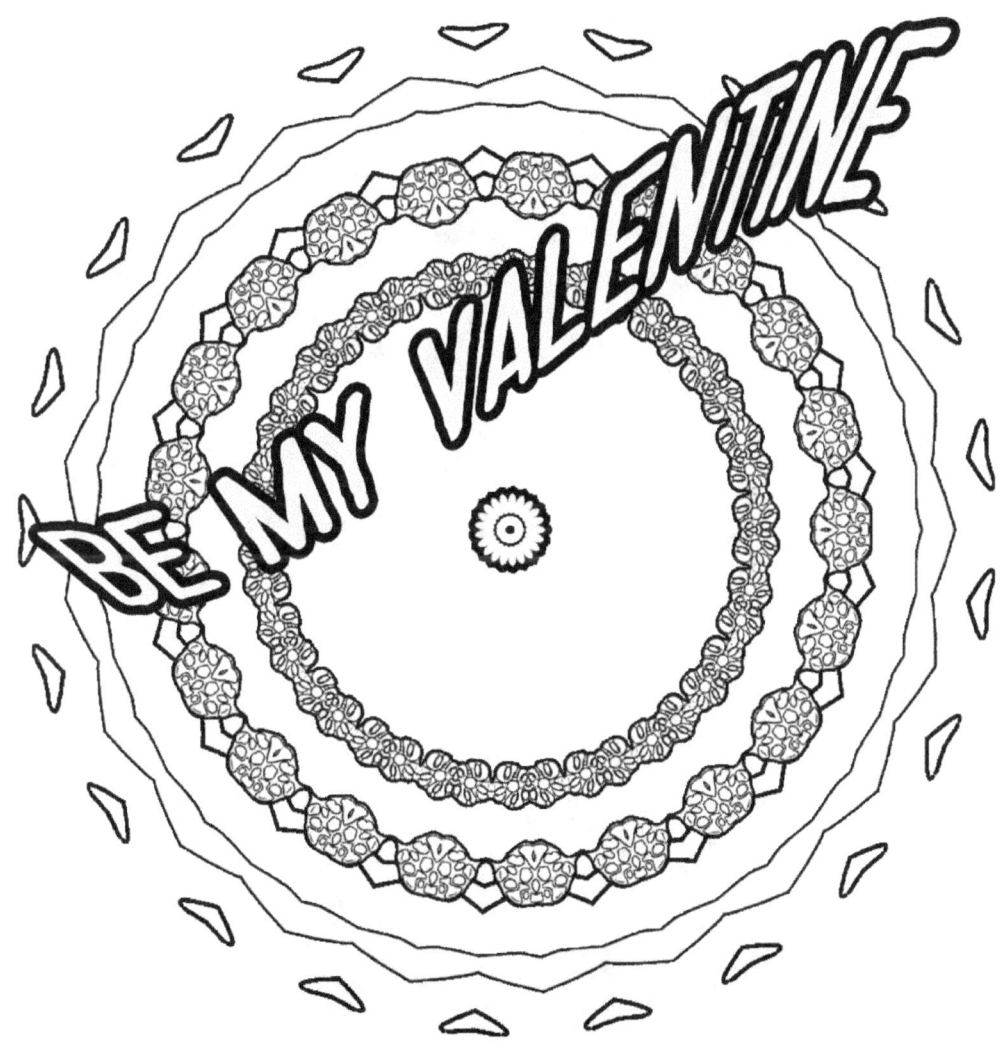

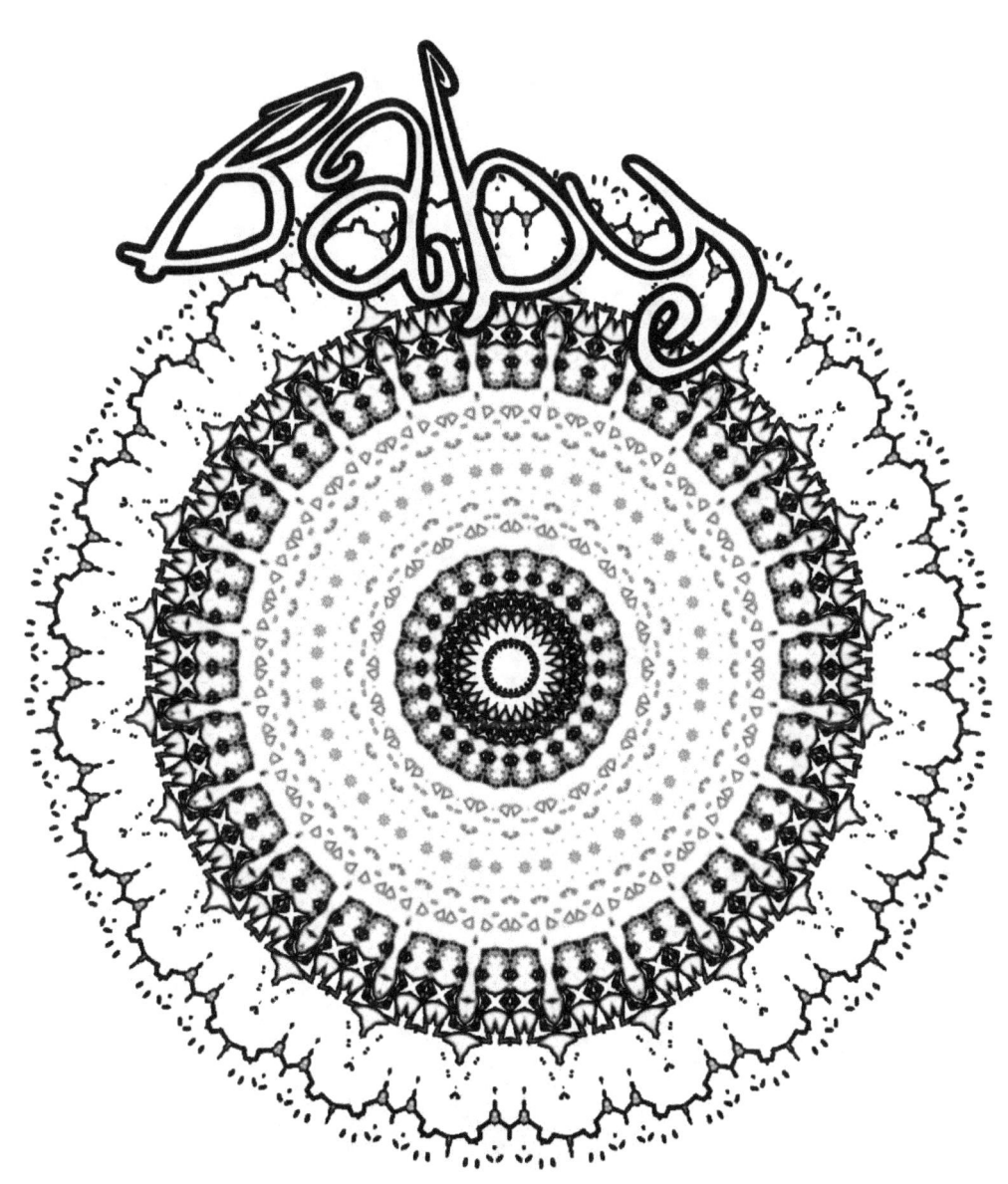

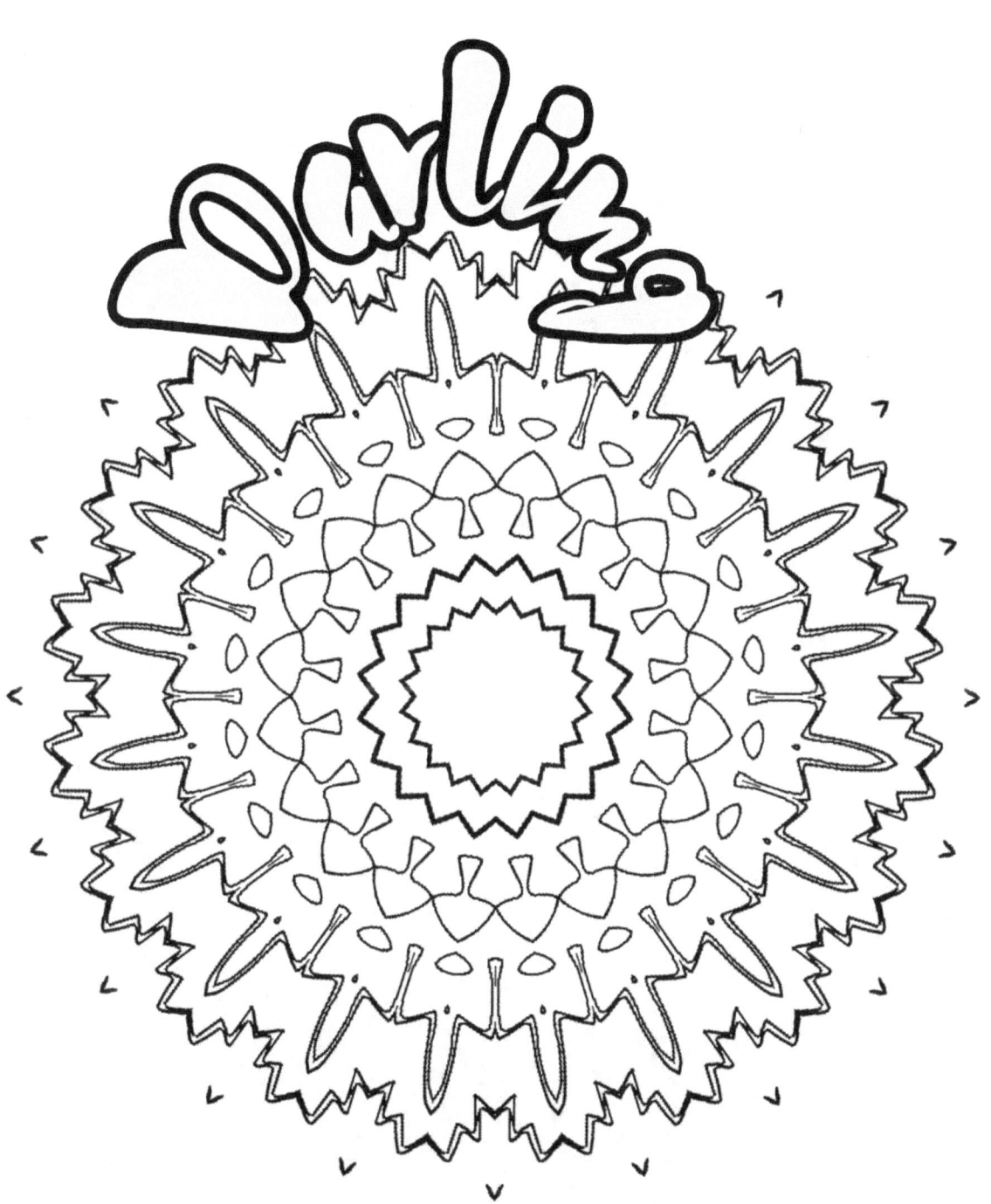

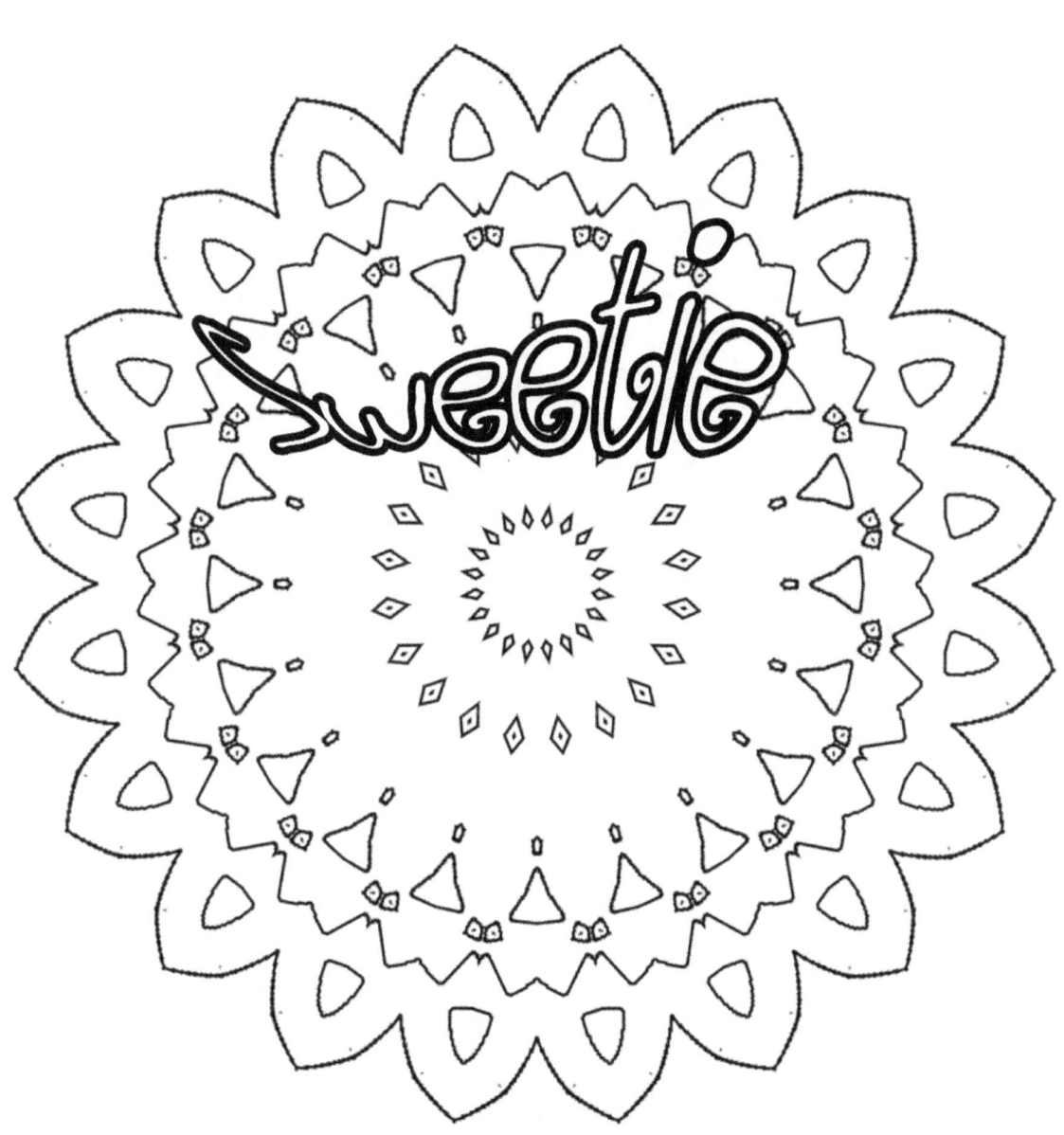

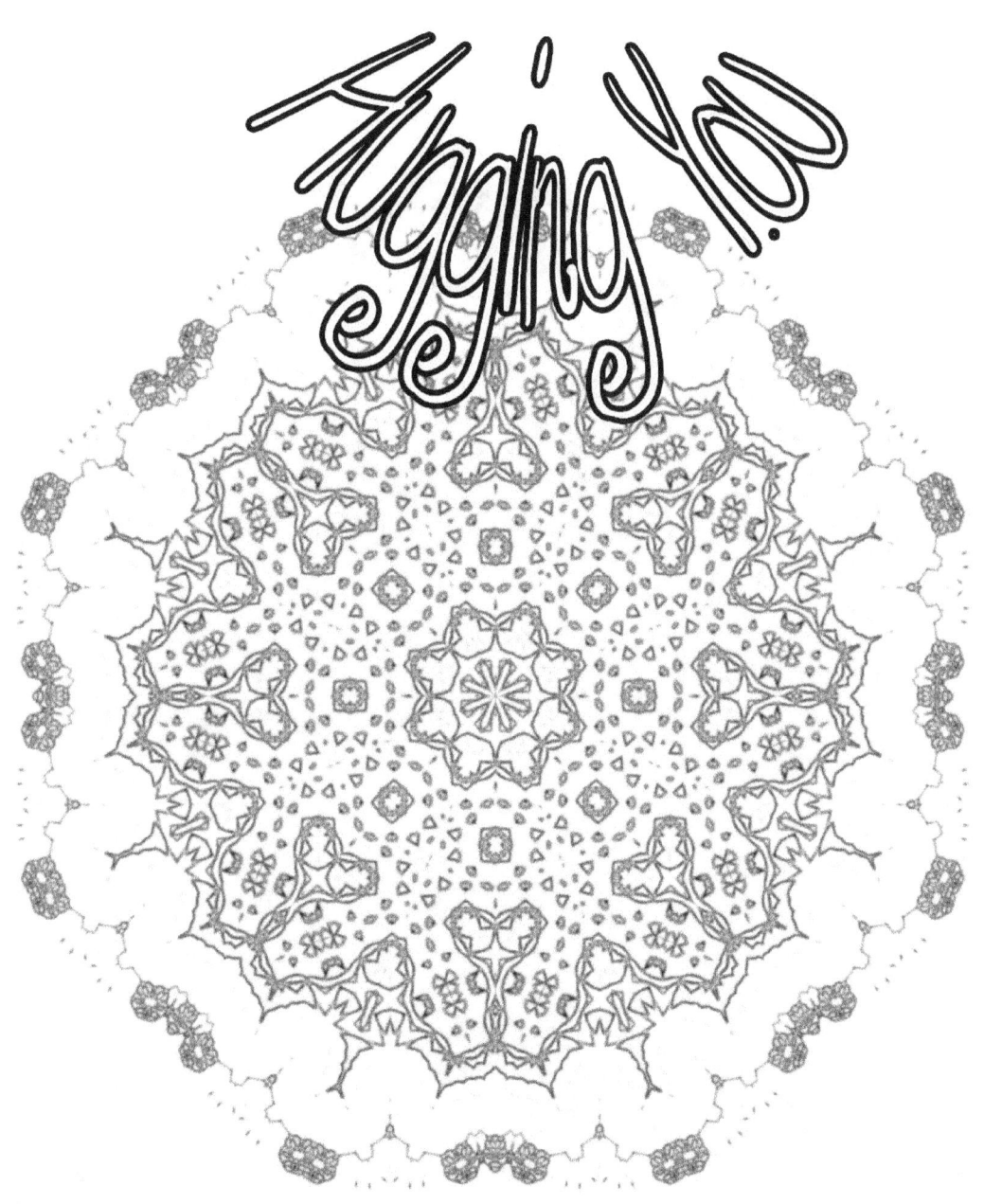

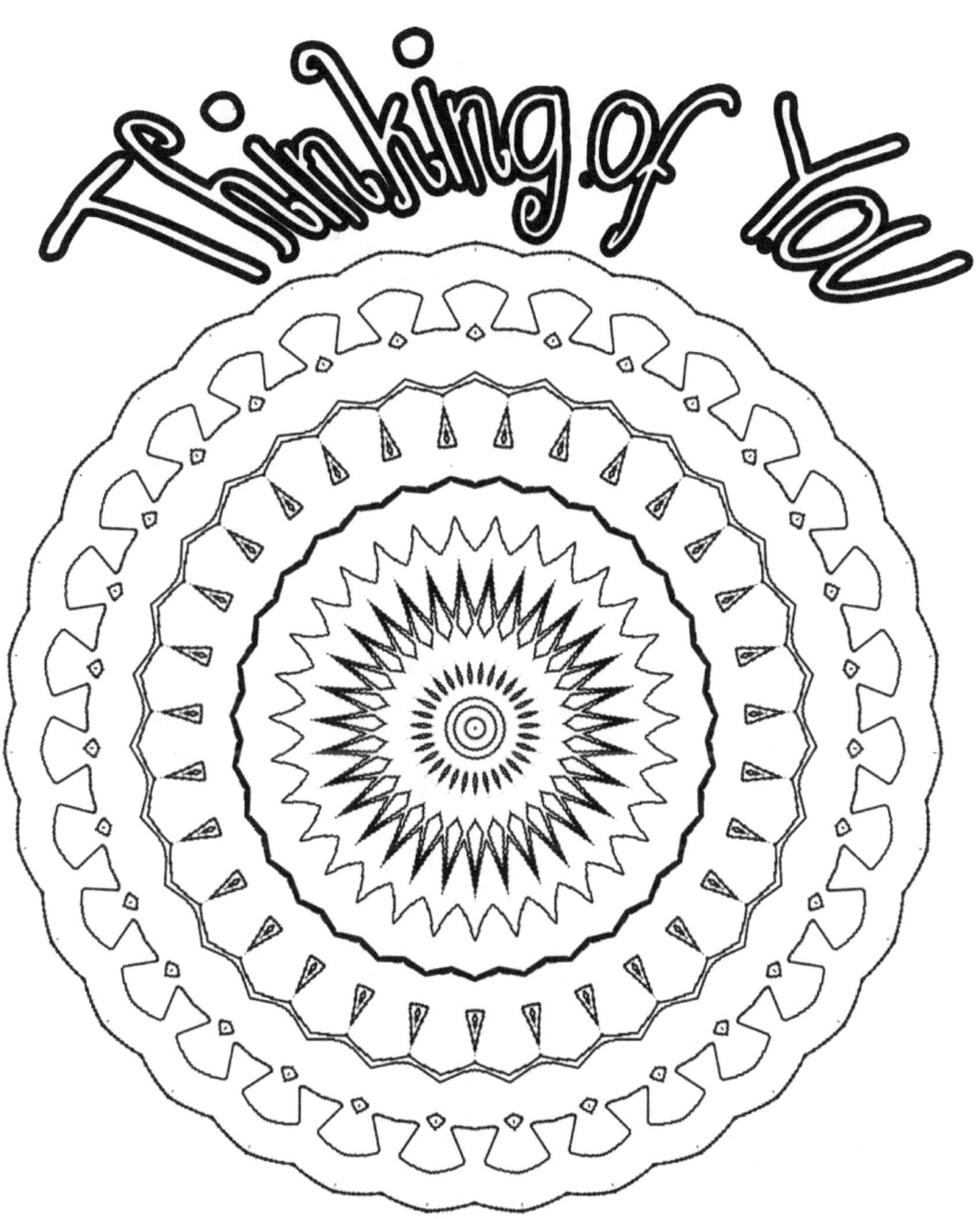

My Beloved One

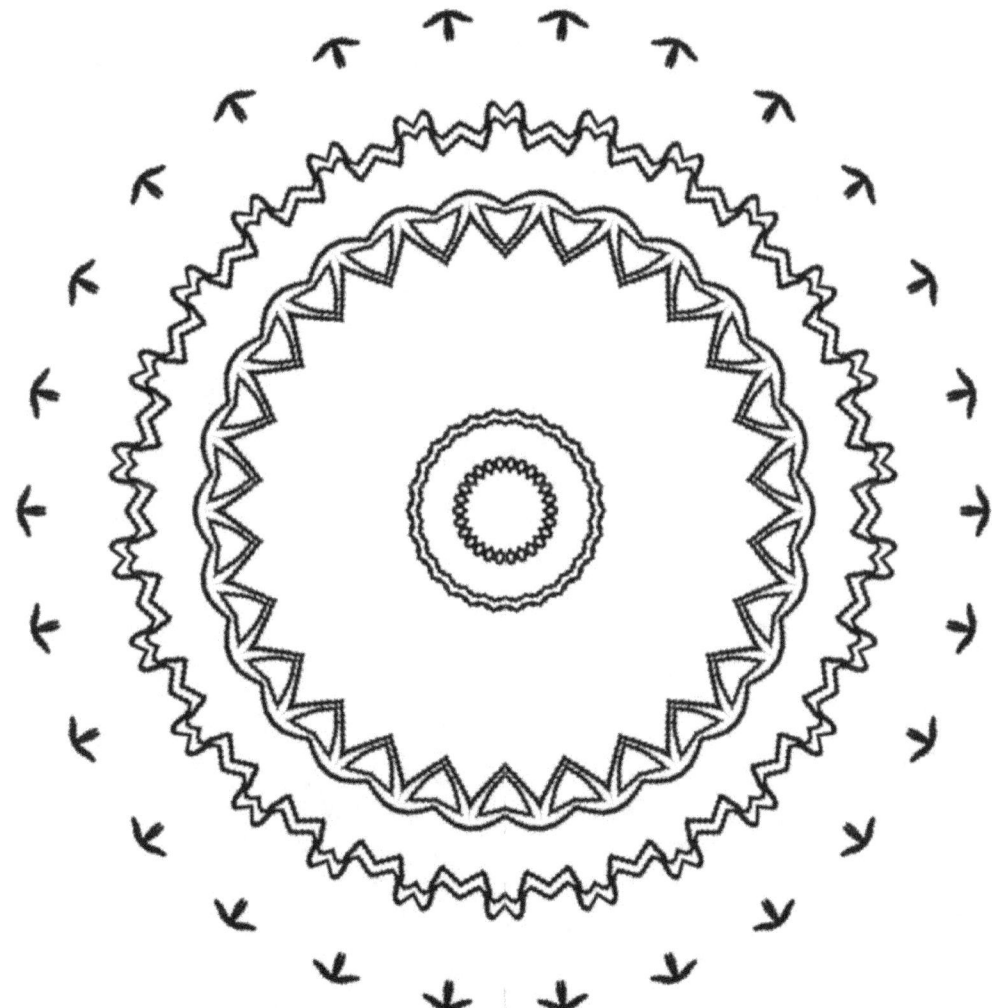

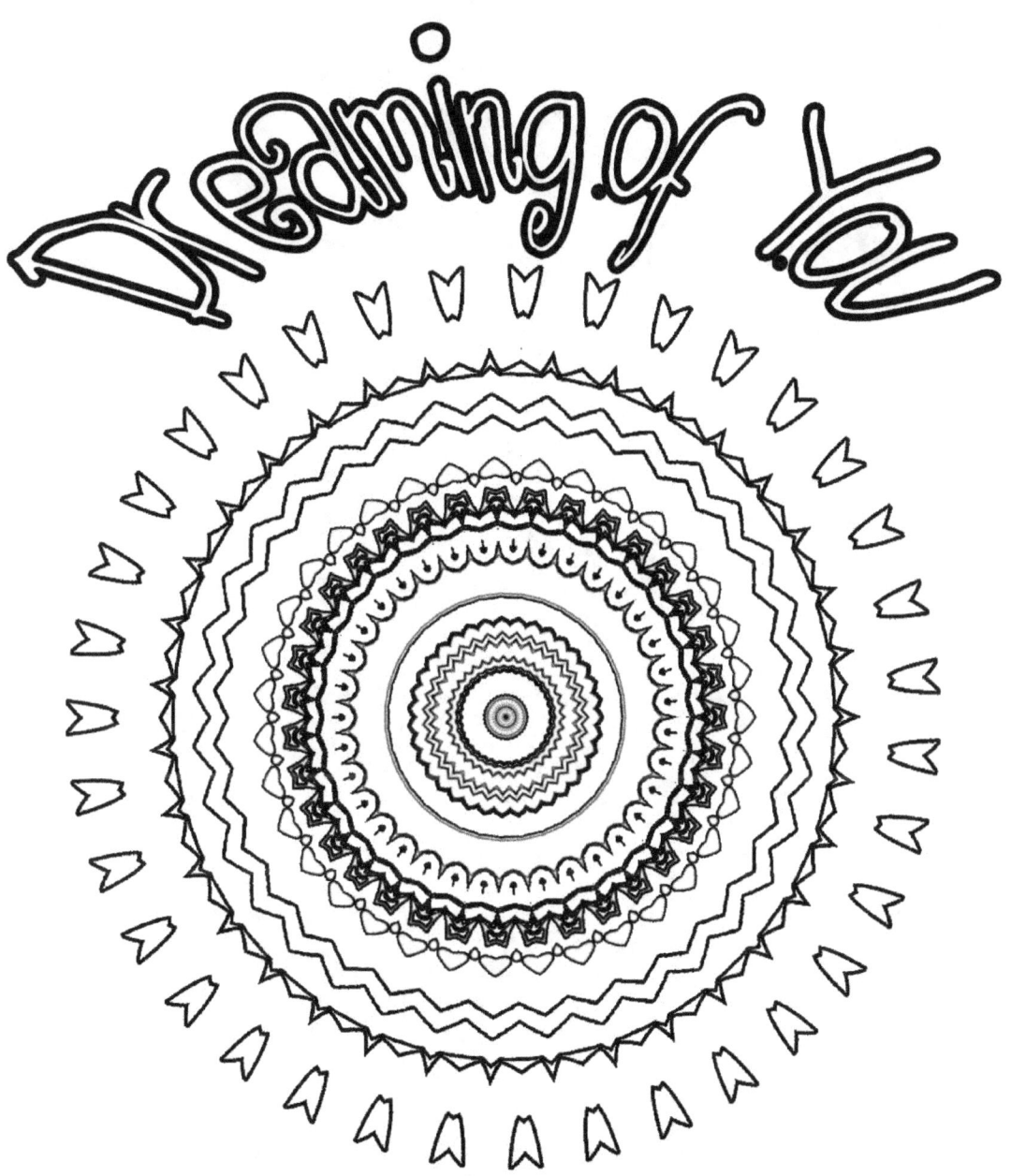

missing you

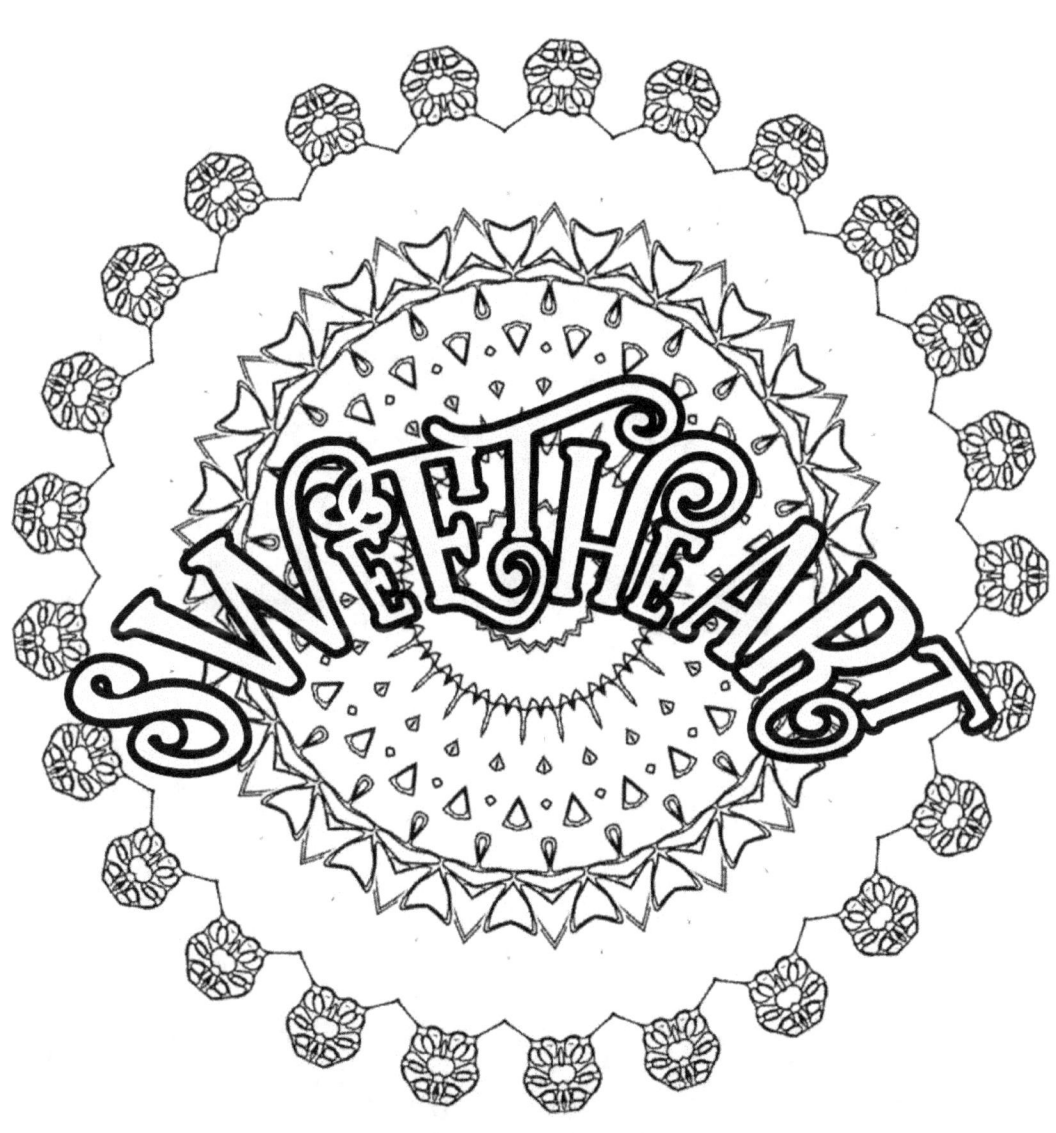

love is like a cloud

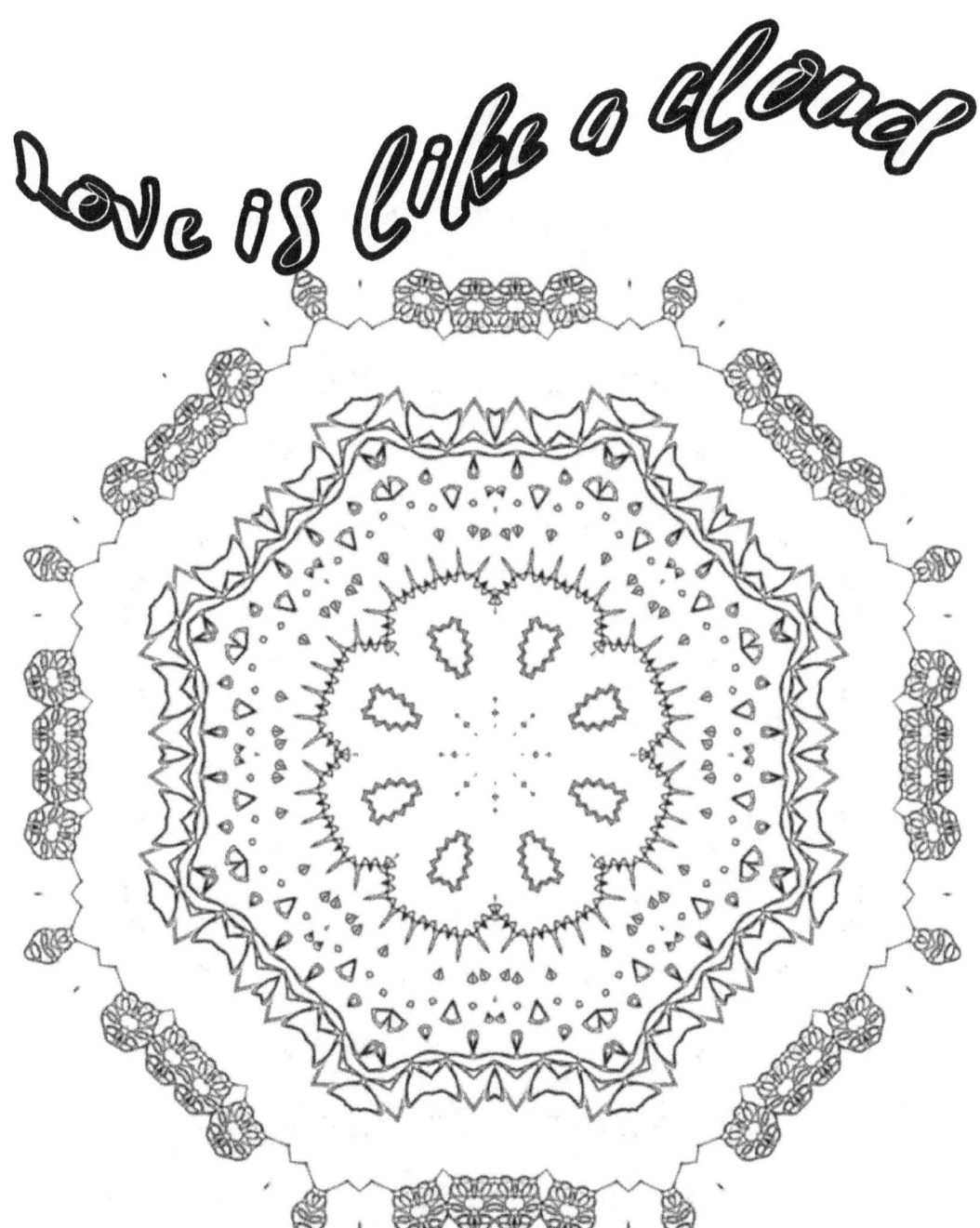

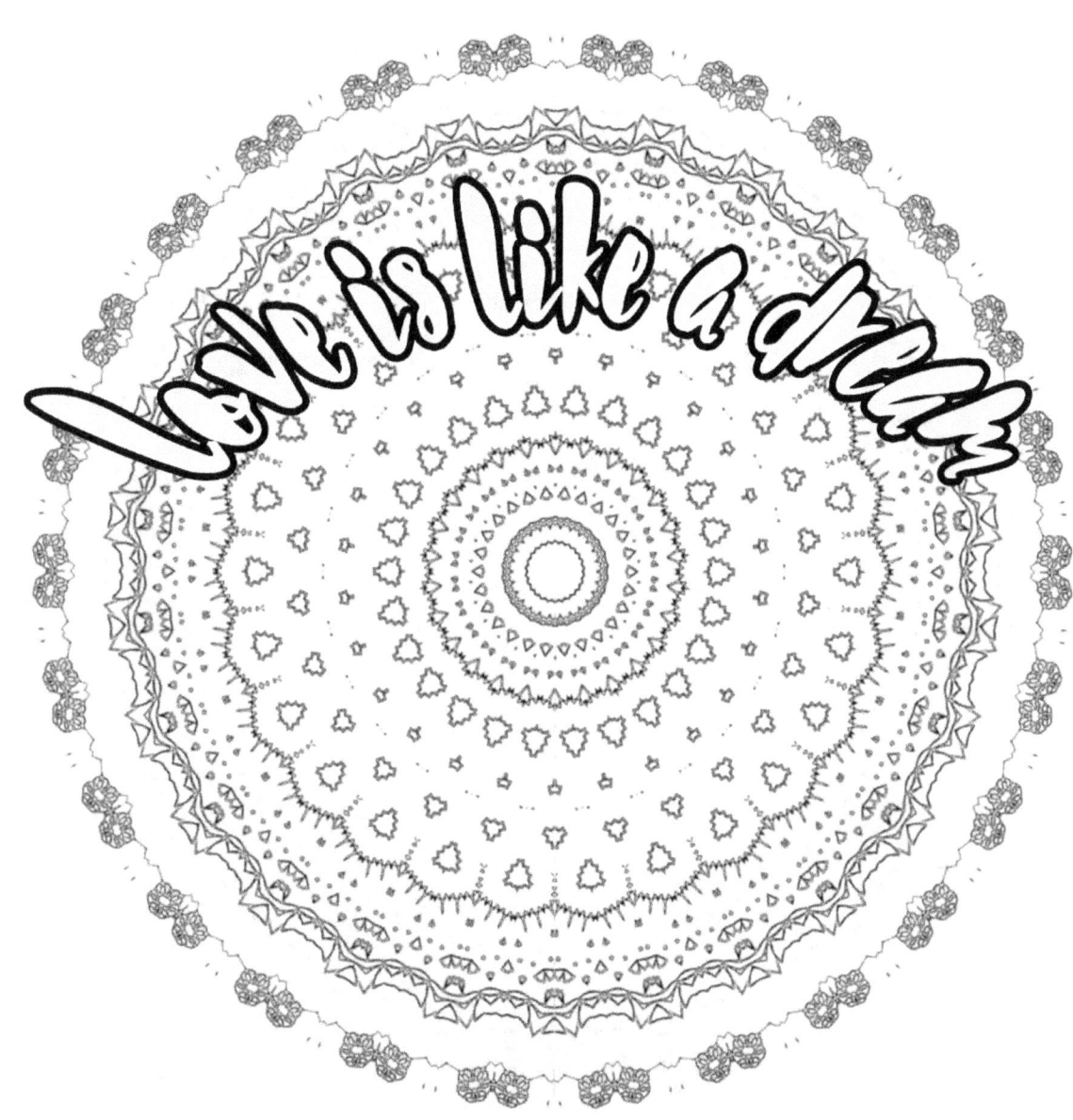

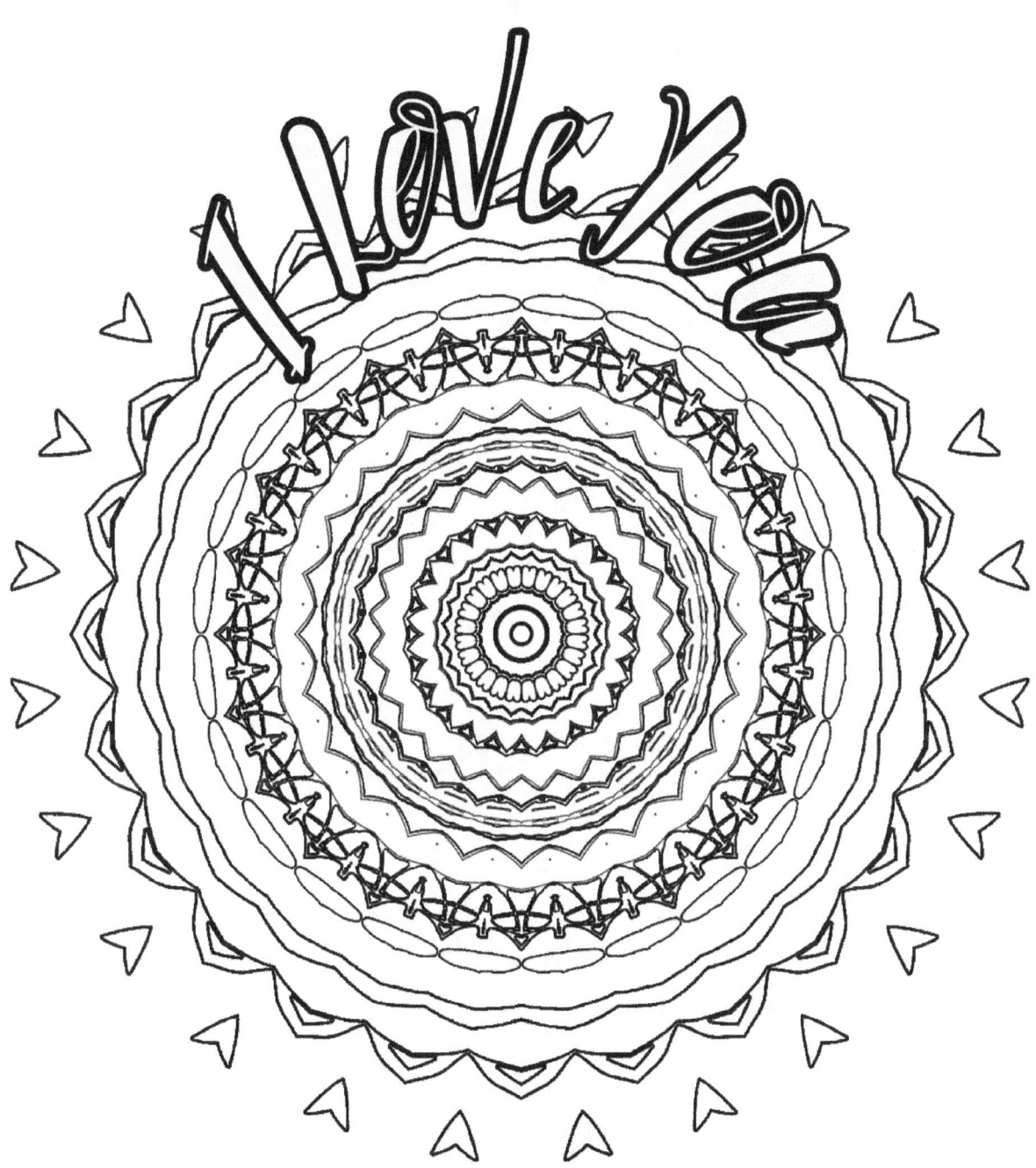

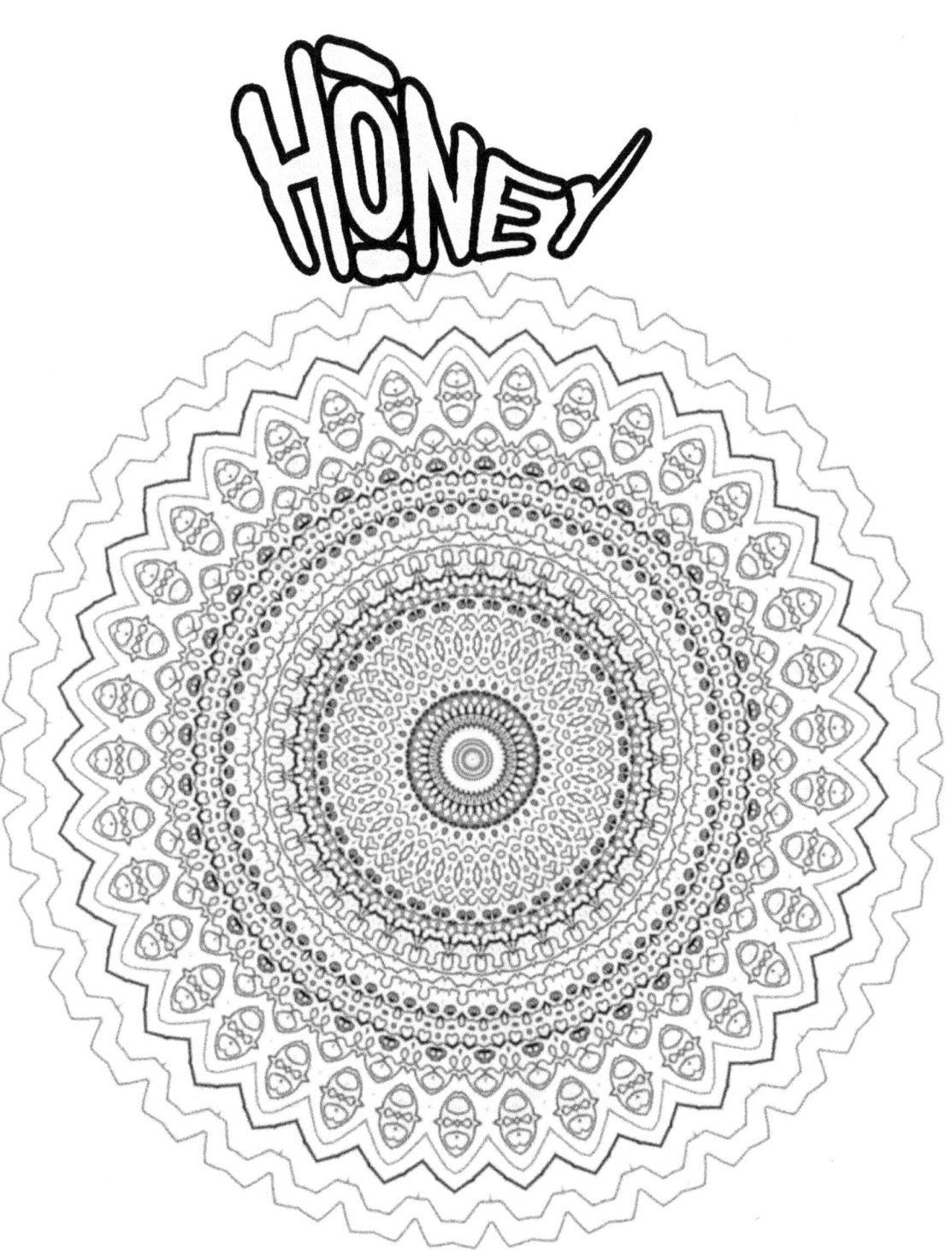

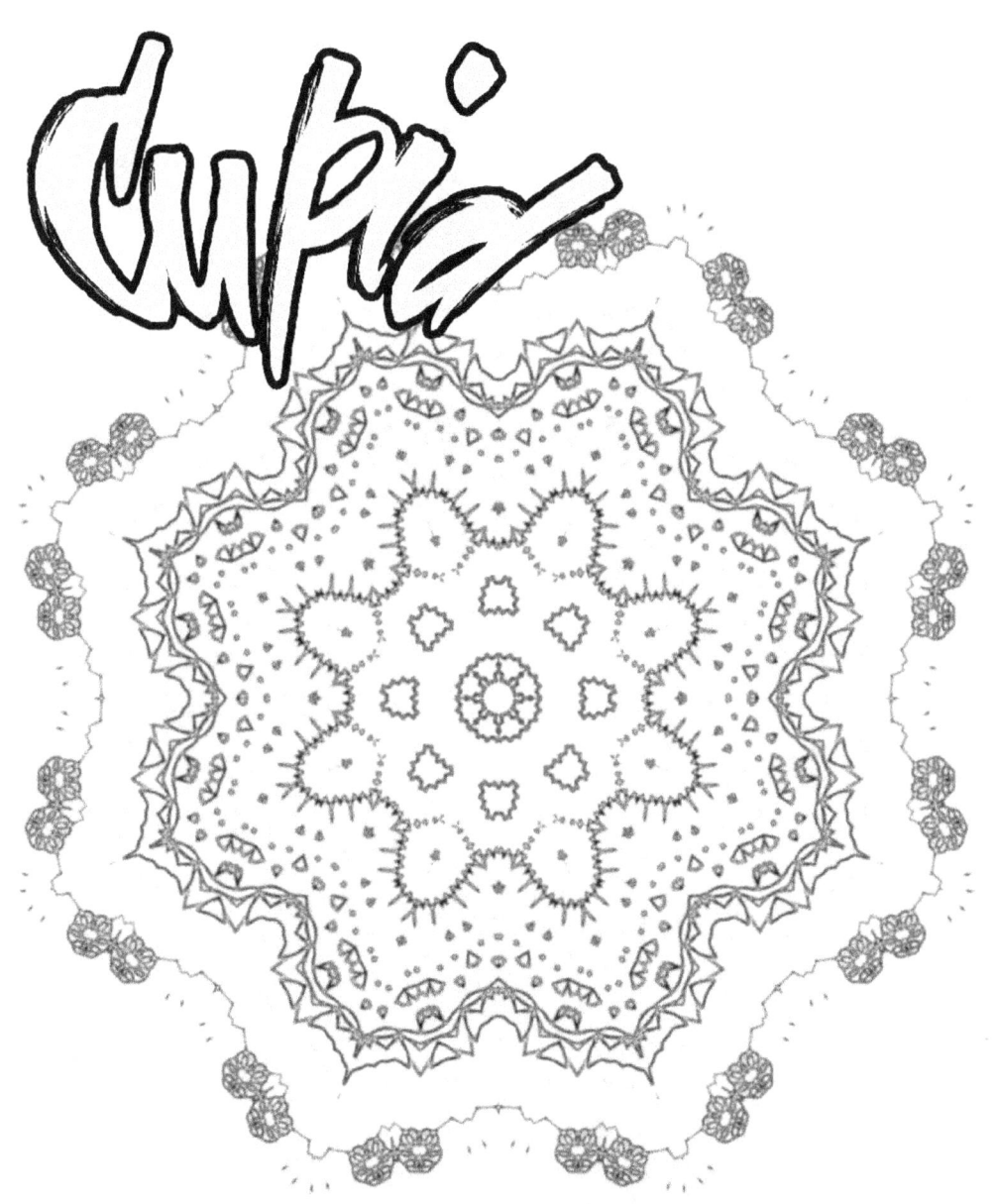

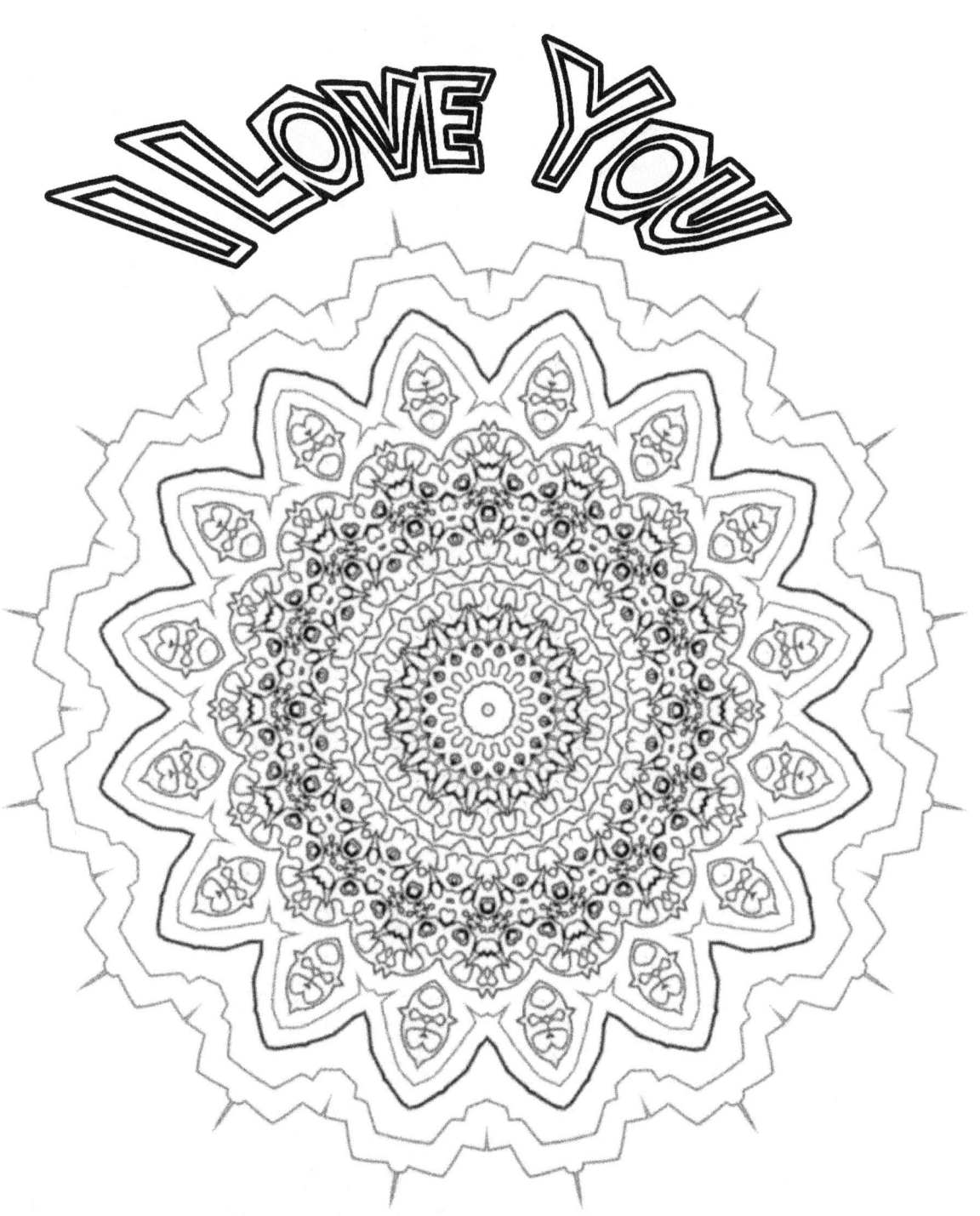